NEDERLANDER THEATRE

UNDER THE DIRECTION OF
JAMES M. NEDERLANDER AND JAMES L. NEDERLANDER

DENA HAMMERSTEIN ROY GABAY RICH ENTERTAINMENT GROUP
DAN FARAH METRO CARD

KING'S LEAVES DAN FRISHWASSER LESLIE GREIF/THOM BEERS SUSAN DIETZ & LENNY BEER
HOWARD HOFFMAN/ANNA CZEKAJ IMPORTANT MUSICALS SHARON KARMAZIN L.G. SCOTT MARTIN MARKINSON

IN ASSOCIATION WITH

KEN GREINER/RUTH HENDEL KRAUSS FREITAG/BOYLE KOENIGSBERG RICK STEINER/BELL-STATON GROUP
PAM PARISEAU

AND

PAPER MILL PLAYHOUSE

PRESENT

ROB McCLURE BRYNN O'MALLEY

AND

TONY DANZA

IN

BOOK
ANDREW BERGMAN

MUSIC & LYRICS
JASON ROBERT

T0079162

BASED ON THE CASTLE ROCK ENTERTAINMENT MOTION PICTURE

ALSO STARRING

DAVID JOSEFSBERG NANCY OPEL MATTHEW SALDIVAR

GEORGE MERRICK CATHERINE RICAFORT
MATT ALLEN TRACEE BEAZER GRADY McLEOD BOWMAN BARRY BUSBY LESLIE DONNA FLESNER
GAELEN GILLILAND ALBERT GUERZON RAYMOND J. LEE JESSICA NAIMY ZACHARY PRINCE
JONALYN SAXER BRENDON STIMSON ERICA SWEANY CARY TEDDER KATIE WEBBER

SCENIC & PROJECTION DESIGN
ANNA LOUIZOS

COSTUME DESIGN
BRIAN HEMESATH

LIGHTING DESIGN
HOWELL BINKLEY

SOUND DESIGN
SCOTT LEHRER & DREW LEVY

WIG & HAIR DESIGNS
CHARLES G. LaPOINTE

PROPS
KATHY FABIAN/
PROPSTAR

CASTING
TELSEY + COMPANY
JUSTIN HUFF, CSA

FLIGHT EFFECTS
FLYING BY FOY

PRODUCTION STAGE MANAGER
MATTHEW DiCARLO

GENERAL MANAGER
ROY GABAY PRODUCTIONS

COMPANY MANAGER
CHRIS ANIELLO

PRESS REPRESENTATIVE
BONEAU/BRYAN-BROWN

ADVERTISING & MARKETING
SPOTCO

PRODUCTION MANAGEMENT
AURORA PRODUCTIONS

ASSOCIATE PRODUCER
DAVID GOLDYN

ORCHESTRATIONS
DON SEBESKY LARRY BLANK JASON ROBERT BROWN CHARLIE ROSEN

MUSIC COORDINATOR
MICHAEL KELLER

MUSIC DIRECTOR
TOM MURRAY

CHOREOGRAPHER
DENIS JONES

DIRECTOR
GARY GRIFFIN

WORLD PREMIERE, PAPER MILL PLAYHOUSE, IN MILLBURN, NJ, ON OCTOBER 6, 2013
MARK S. HOEBEE, PRODUCING ARTISTIC DIRECTOR, TODD SCHMIDT, MANAGING DIRECTOR

By special arrangement with Warner Bros. Theatre Ventures, Inc. Original Cast Album available on UM®

ISBN 978-1-4950-2250-0

7777 W. BLUEMOUND RD. P.O. BOX 13819 MILWAUKEE, WI 53213

I LOVE BETSY

Music and Lyrics by
JASON ROBERT BROWN

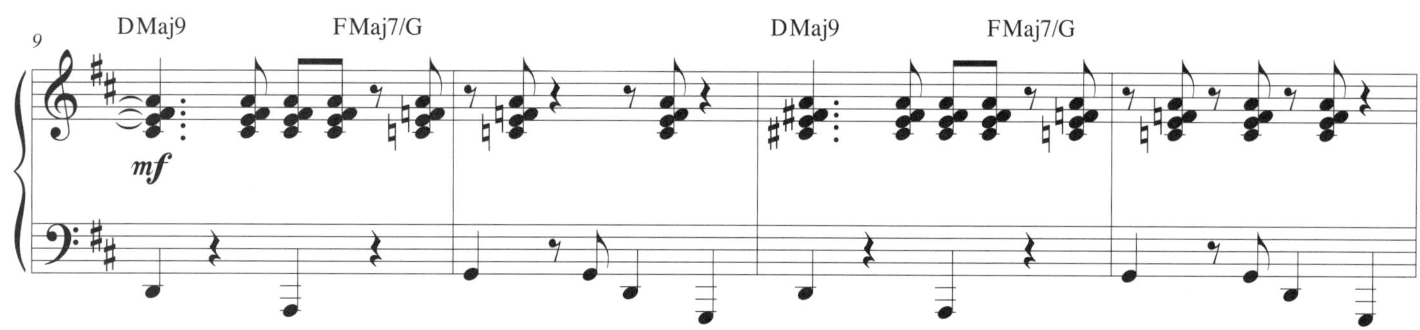

17
DMaj9
tax - is, I like trains. I like Brook - lyn when it rains. But I love
mp
21
Em7♭5/D
Bet - sy. I like
25
C9
Gm6/A
walk - ing af - ter dark. I like jogs in Pros - pect Park. But I love
29
DMaj9
Bet - sy. I like

33
Am7/D
Ab7b5
Shake Shack, I like MO - MA, And New Jer - sey's ripe a - ro - ma, The pa -
37
GMaj9
C13
rades when I see 'em, And e - ven the D - M - V,
And the Brook -
41
DMaj7/A
Bm7(11)
B7#9
- lyn Bridge by bike...
Heck, there's lots of stuff I like,
44
E13
A13
But I love Bet - sy,
And she loves

47
DMaj9
FMaj7/G
DMaj9
FMaj7/G
me!
f
51
DMaj9
FMaj7/G
DMaj9 N.C.
She likes
55
DMaj9
Em7/D
DMaj9
hock - ey. No, I swear!
She likes guys with thin - ning hair!
And I love
mf
59
Gm6/D
Bet - sy!
She likes

63
C9
Gm6/A
piz - za and Chi - nese,
Lou - bou - tins and mac and cheese!
God, I love
67
DMaj9
Em7/D
DMaj9
Bet - sy!
She likes
71
Am7/D
A♭7♭5
swim - ming, writ - ing let - ters,
She likes watch - ing dou - ble head - ers,
She drinks
75
GMaj9
C13
bour - bon and sa - ke and e - ven likes *Rock - y III.*
I'm a - mazed

79
DMaj7/A
Bm7(11)
B7♯9
and I'm im - pressed, But the thing that I love best Is I love
83
E13
GMaj9/A N.C.
Bet - sy... And she loves me!
f
Lightly swinging, in 2
87
B♭Maj9
Five years! I've been in love with Bet - sy for
mf
91
FMaj7/A
five years. I can't be - lieve she stuck with me!

95
Fm6/A♭
Fm6
Dm7♭5
G7♯5
What kind of luck have I got To keep some-one like her a-
3
3
99
CMaj9
CMaj9♯11
round?
3
3
103
B♭Maj9
Ten years...
My Mom's been dead al-read-y for
3
3
107
FMaj7/A
ten years!
So since she put that curse on me...
3
3

111
Dm7♭5
No! There's no curse. It's not a curse. For-get I said "curse." The point is, It's
cresc.
115
Em7♭5
been long e - nough. Now it's time to grow up! Mom's in the
Samba
119
Em7/A
A7♭9
Em7/A
A7♭9
ground...
And look what I
sub. mp
cresc.
123
Em7/A
A13
found!
I like
ff

127
DMaj9
Em7/D
DMaj9
dancing on the pier. I like Broadway (once a year) But I love
mf
131
Em7♭5/D
Betsy! I like
135
C9
Gm6/A
3
visits to the zoo! I like opera! That's not true, But I love
139
DMaj9
Em7/D
DMaj9
Betsy! It's been

143
Am7/D
A♭7♭5
five years and I'm ready! Get the sparklers and confetti! Give a
147
GMaj9
C13
wink to the waiter and summon the maitre d'! Just like
151
DMaj7/A
Bm7
B7♯9
Jay-Z and Beyoncé, I will make her my fiancée! I love
155
E9
Betsy! I love
f

159
Gm D7 Gm D7 Gm D7 Gm D7
Bet - sy!
I love
163
D/A Em7/A
Bet - sy...
And Bet - sy
ff
Broadly
167
D6 GMaj7
loves me! I'm a schmuck and Bet - sy loves me. Does-n't mat-ter what I
mf
171
D/A G A/G D/F♯ Gsus2 D/A A
do, I know it's true, I could nev - er live with - out her! Bet - sy

175
D6
GMaj7
C7♯11
loves me. It's a - maz - ing, Bet - sy loves me! And to -
rit.
Tempo I
179
D6/A
night I'm gon - na show her Just how proud I am to know
sub. mf
(build...)
182
G♯m7♭5
her! There's no dan - ger, there's no dra - ma, There's no
(build...)
Go!
185
GMaj9
curse and there's no Ma - ma! Put my prob - lems in the past!
f

188
C9♯11
I'm a grown - up man at
192
D6/A
last!
I'm the luck - i - est guy from the
mf
196
G♯m7♭5
Bronx to the Is - land, So laugh if you wan - na, This whole town is gon - na see
199
GMaj9
C13
That I love

203
D6/A
Bet - sy!
Sor - ry, Ma - ma, I love
f
207
G(add2)/A
Bet - sy!
And she
(r.h.)
211
DMaj9
FMaj7/G
DMaj9
FMaj7/G
loves me!
ff
215
DMaj9
FMaj7/G
E♭Maj7♯11
D
sfz

NEVER GET MARRIED

Music and Lyrics by
JASON ROBERT BROWN

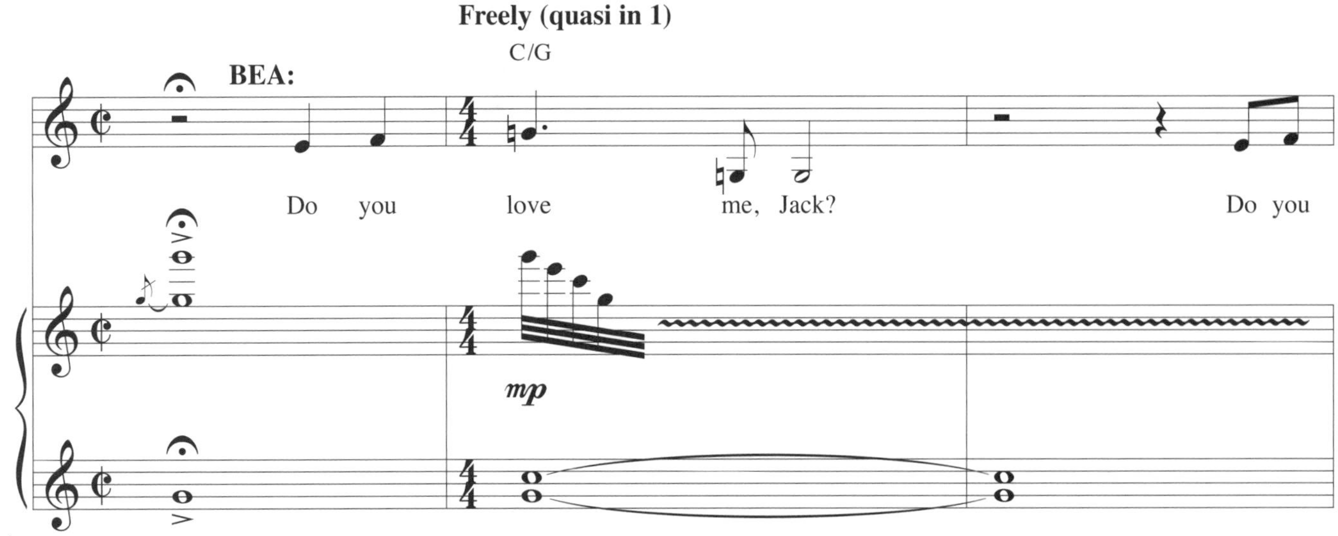

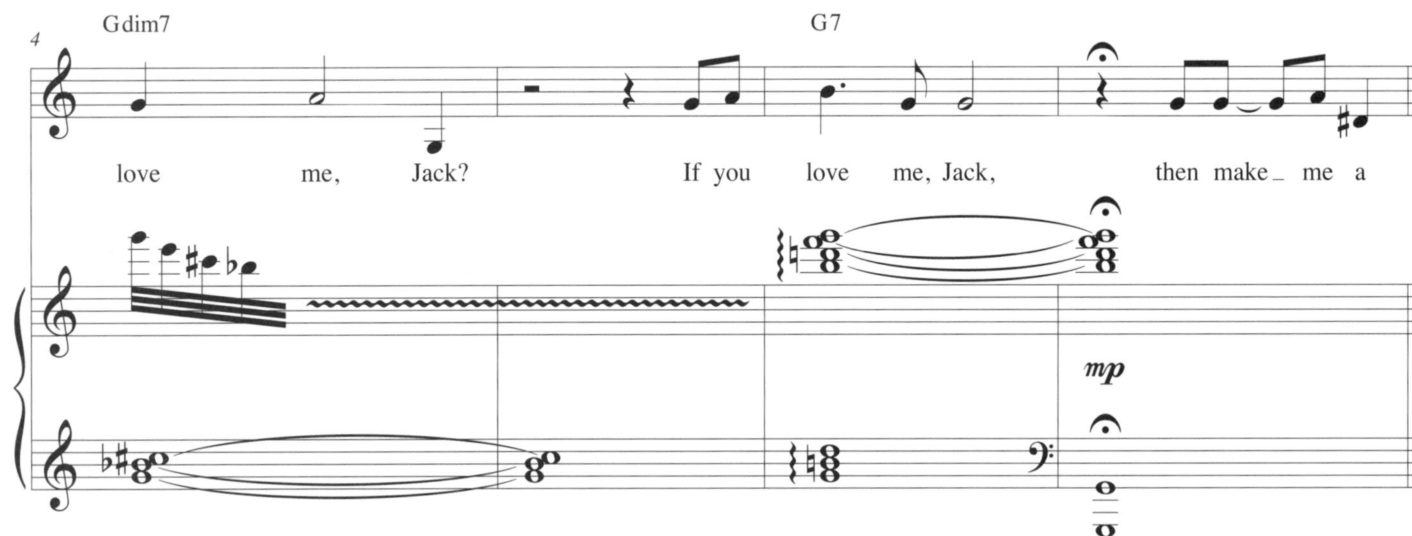

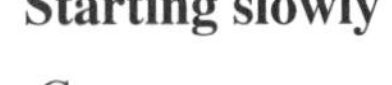

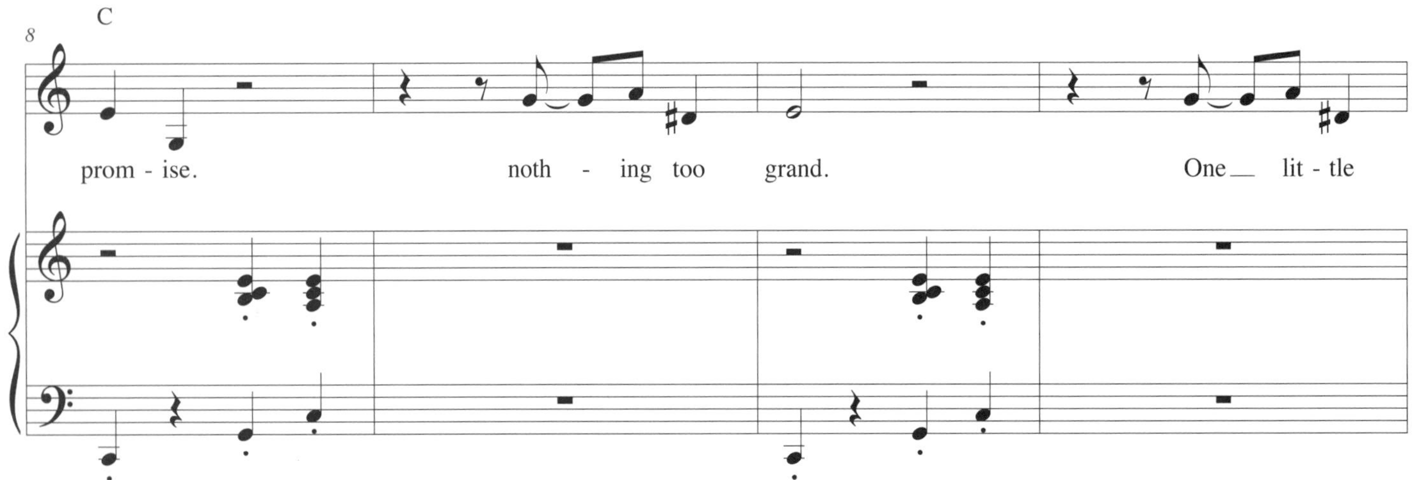

12
C13
prom - ise for Mom - my. No, here take my hand. Nev - er get
16
F6 B♭9 C/G
mar - ried. That's all that I ask. How can I
20
D7 C(add2)/E Fm6 D7/F♯ G7 F(add2)/A A♯m6 G7/B
know that you'll love me for - ev - er, un - less I'm sure that you will nev - er get
accel.
24
C C6 CMaj7 G7♯5 C C6 CMaj7 G7♯5
mar - ried. On - ly be - cause No oth - er

28
C C7♯5 C G7♯5 C C13
wom - an could love you like your mom - my does. You can just
32
F6 F♯dim7 C/G A7
toss me in the Hud - son, I'll be food for the fish, But
36
D13 F(add2)/G N.C.
don't ig - nore a moth - er's dy - ing w… Nev - er get
rit.
40
D♭ D♭6 D♭Maj7 A♭7♯5 D♭ D♭6 D♭Maj7 A♭7♯5
mar - ried. That's what I said! Sure, you'll be
a tempo

D♭ D♭6 D♭Maj7 D♭6 D♭ D♭6 D♭13
laugh - ing and danc - ing the sec - ond I'm dead,
G♭6 C♭9
But I will be watch - ing! What else can I
D♭Maj7/A♭ E♭7 D♭/F
do? And if you find some girl and
G♭m6 E♭9/G A♭7 G♭(add2)/B♭ Bm A♭7/C
think I'll soft - en I'll claw my way out of the cof - fin and

56
D
DMaj7
D6
A7♯5/C♯
D
DMaj7
D6
A7♯5/C♯
crush her! Nev - er mind how! So, when your
f (straight 8ths)
60
D
D13
mom - my says, "Prom - ise," You prom - ise right now! And if you
64
G6
G♯dim7
D/A
Bm7
think I might be jok - ing just take a look at this nurse. So
mp
68
E7
F♯m7
Gdim7
E7/G♯
A7
D6
N.C.
don't you un - der - es - ti - mate a moth - er's curse! No,
f

E9 D/F♯ Gm(Maj7) G♯m7♭5 A7
72
nev - er un - der - es - ti - mate a moth - er's... Do you
rit.
Freely (quasi in 1)
D/A Adim7
76
love me, Jack? Do you love me, Jack? If you
mp
A7/C♯ A7
80
love me, Jack You'll nev - er get
p
ff
Heavy (in 4)
(Dictated)
D5 D
83
mar - ried!
(dies)
ff
rit.
sffz

ANYWHERE BUT HERE

Music and Lyrics by
JASON ROBERT BROWN

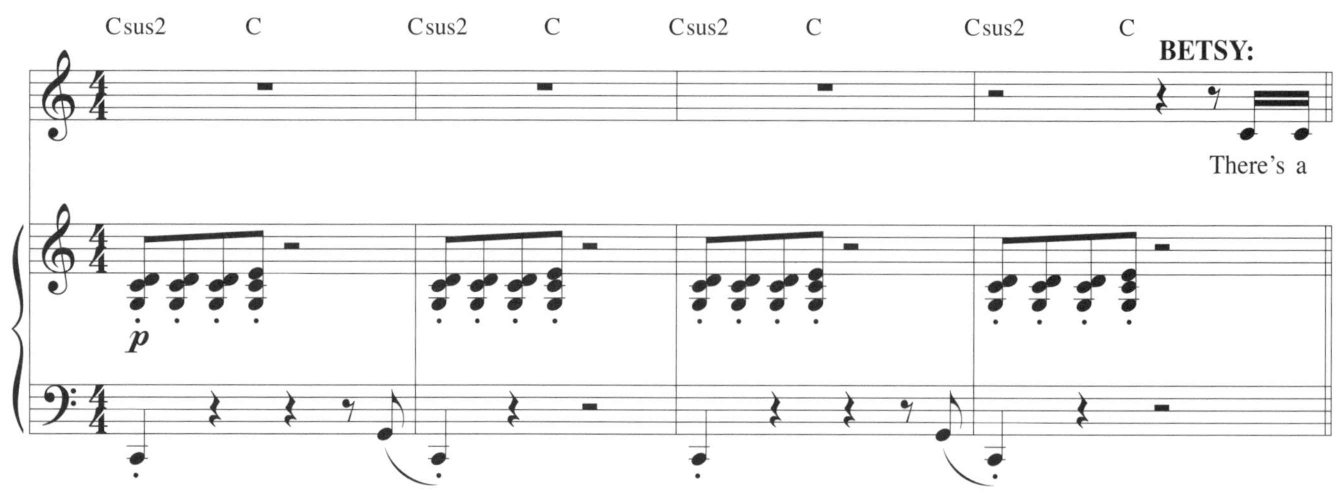

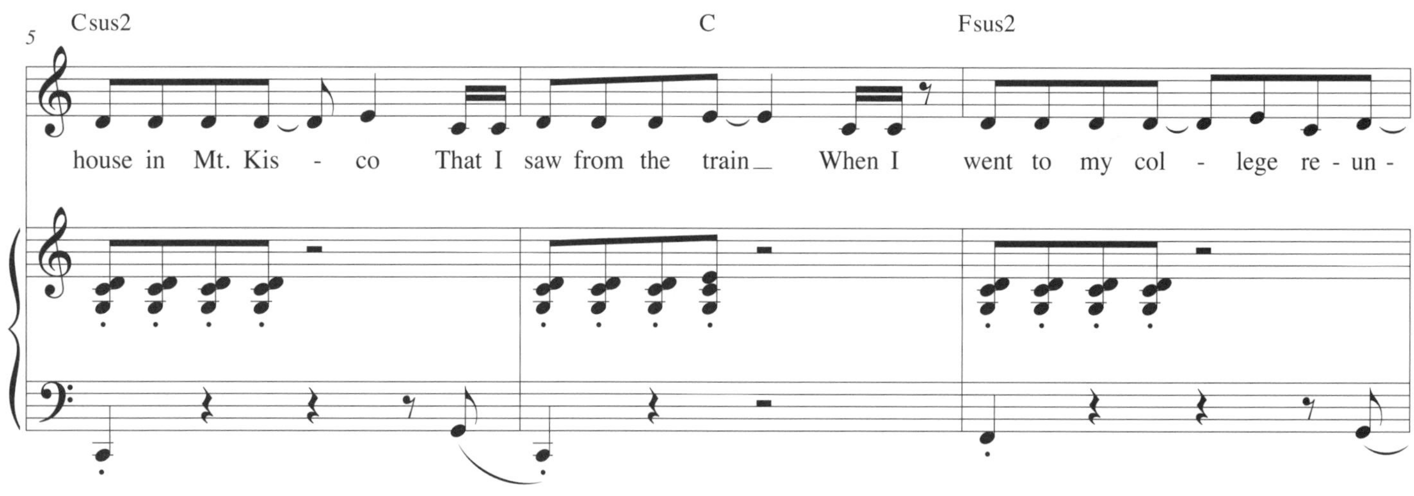

11
Fsus2
G7sus
Csus2
C
Em11
saw there were swings in the yard.
And I looked at that swing - set, And with-
14
Fsus2
out an - y warn - ing I was to - tal - ly griev - ing Like a wom - an in mourn - ing And
17
D/E
Em7
D/E
Bm7
E7/G♯
Am7
all that I want - ed Was a house in Mt. Kis - co With a rust - y old swing set
20
F2
Dsus
D
For our ba - by to ride.
Some -

Freely
23
G/C
G(add2)/B
Am7(add4)
Fsus2
- where in New York, Winds _ are blow - ing. Win - ter's go - ing In - to spring. _ Ev -
mp
27
Em7(add4)
Bm7
C(add2)
Dsus
D
- 'ry - where you look, Things _ are grow - ing– An - y - where _ but here. _ Some -
colla voce
mf
Poco tempo
31
G/C
G(add2)/B
Am7(add4)
- where in New York, At - oms split - ting, Lov - ers sit - ting On _
34
Fsus2
Em7(add4)
Bm7
_ a swing. _ Strange _ though it may seem, Men _ com - mit - ting! An -

37
Csus2
C(add2)/D
Gsus2
G
Gsus2
G
G5
- y - where but here.
And I've
40
Csus2(♯4)
C(add2)
G(add2)/B
Gsus
G
been pa - tient. We've been "dat - ing"
mf
44
Csus2(♯4)
C(add2)
G(add2)/B
G
Gsus
G
five years, No com - plaints from me.
48
Csus2(♯4)
C(add2)
G(add2)/B
Gsus
G
I've been qui - et, I've been wait - ing,

52
Am7(add4) G(add2)/B C(add2) Am7 G(add2)/B C Csus2/D C/D
know-ing, like I Know my name, That you and I are meant to be, And some-
56
G/C C G/B Am/B G/B Am7 Am9(add4) Am7
-where in New York, That would mat-ter, That would make things crys-
59
F9#11 Em7 G5/D C(add2)
-tal clear. An-y oth-er life, We'd
8va
loco
62
G/B Am7 Am7(add4) D7sus Gsus2 G
be sit-ting An-y-where but here.

Gsus2 G GMaj9 GMaj7 F(add2)/G GMaj7
66
Em11 Csus2 C(add2)
69
BETSY:
Look at them, on their way, March-ing arm in arm,
8vb
Em11 C/D Gsus2 Gsus G
73
Read-y for what-ev-er lies in store.
(8vb)
loco
Em11 D/F♯ F(add2)/G
77
Look at us, smart as hell, Deep in love, do-ing well.

81
C/E
F(add2)
B♭9
Still you've got one foot out the door! Don't
85
E♭Maj9
A♭7#11
we de-serve... Don't I de-serve more?
3
89
C(add2)/D
C6
G/B
Csus2
C/B
C
Csus2/D
'Cause some-
93
C(add2)
G/B
Am7(add4)
G(add4)
days in New York, I'm in-clined to change my mind and Dis-

96
F9#11
Em7
Dsus
C(add2)
- ap - pear. One day in New York, You
8va
loco
99
G/B
C(add2)
Cm9(Maj9)
might find You'll look for me, And I will be
103
Am7(add4)
G/B
C(add2)
Am7(add4)
G/B
Am7/D
An - y - where But here.
rall.
Poco meno
108
Gsus2
G
C6(no3)
CMaj7(no3)
F9
F9#11
G
rit.

WHEN YOU SAY VEGAS

Music and Lyrics by
JASON ROBERT BROWN

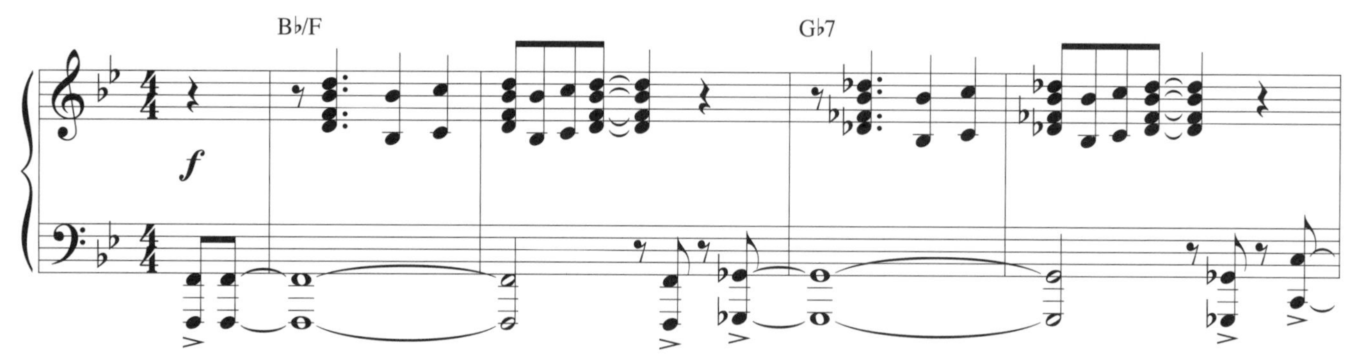

12
Gm
Gm(Maj7)
Gm7
You're say - in' dia - mond rings And all the things That
15
C9
G♭7♭5
B♭6/F
lit - tle girls dream of. You're hear - in' bells go ring ding
3
18
G7♯5
G7/B
Cm9
ding for me and you In Las Ve - gas, the land
22
N.C.
F7
where dreams come true. When
3
3
3
3

N.C.
Am7♭5
you say, "Ve - gas!", You're say - in', "yes!"
D7
Gm
Gm(Maj7)
Gm7
You're talk - in' Broad - way shows, De - sign - er clothes, And wow,
C9
G♭7♭5
B♭6/F
babe, that's quite a dress. On - ly suck - ers go to Fox -
G7♯5
G7/B
- woods, Get a clue, And come to

37
Cm9
E♭/F
B♭
Ve - gas,
the land
where dreams
come true!
40
A♭/B♭
B♭9♯5
Put on your tux,
dress her up
to her
43
E♭Maj13
E♭Maj9
C9sus
mo - lars;
Show her you roll
46
C7♭5
F13
with the high
-
est
roll - ers!

49
Cm6/D D7 Gm Gm(Maj7)
Flash some cash, snag a front-row seat, It's a night that she won't for - get.
52
Gm7 C7 B♭/C Cm7♭5 C7
You might be in the de - sert, kid, But a girl
55
Cm7 B♭/D E♭ Edim F13 N.C.
can still get wet! I'm jok - ing! Hey! When
57
Am7♭5
you say, "Ve - gas!" You're say - in', "Bring it on! Bring it on!"

60
Cm6/D D7 Gm Gm(Maj7) Gm7
— You're — say - in', "Fill my heart — with beaut - y and art — And don't —
63
C9 G♭9♭5 B♭6/F
— quit be - fore I'm gone!" — You can see Miss Li - za Mi - nel - li, Miss Bar - bra
66
Fm6/G G7
Streis-and Or you can just miss Ce - line Di - on! — You're — say - in', "Deal —
(Half-Time)
69
Cm7 C♯dim7 B♭6/D
— me a flush!" "Hey, — sor - ry, Mis - ter! How should I know that

Fm6/G
G7♯5
Cm7(add4)
E♭/F
F7/E♭
strip - per's your sis - ter?" Cash in your chips and thank the stars a - bove
Cm6/D
D7
G7
Cm9
B♭(add2)/D
That you're in V - E -
E♭6
Edim7
F13
E13 F13
G - A - S,
And that spells
B♭6
B♭6/D
E♭
F13
N.C.
love!
mf

85
A♭6/B♭
A♭9♯5/B♭
Find a ma - chine and start yank - in' that
87
E♭6
Fm
F♯m Cm7/G
C9sus
lev - er.
Chanc - es are swell
90
C7♭5
E♭maj7/F
F13
you'll get luck - y for - ev - er!
(gliss through
whole measure)
93
Cm6/D
D7
TOMMY:
Ve - gas is, was, and al - ways will be The

95
Gm
Gm(Maj7)
Gm7
JOHNNY:
hot - test of all hot spots. There's
97
Gm/C
B♭/C
Cm7♭5
C7
some guys been here fif - ty years And they're still
99
Cm7
B♭/D
E♭
Edim
F13
N.C.
ALL 3:
shov - ing things in slots! What am I talk - in' a - bout! When you say, "Ve - gas!",
102
Am7♭5
Am7♭5/D
D♭13♯11
You're say - in', "The sky's al - ways blue!"

(Half-Time)
Cm9
C♯dim7
105
JOHNNY:
TOMMY:
BUDDY:
Lon - don's too old,
Cleve - land ain't pret - ty, And we've got
B♭6/D
Fm/G
G7♯5
107
ALL 3:
nic - er hook - ers Than Jer - sey Cit - y! There's
Cm7(add4)
E♭/F
F7/E♭
109
a whole lot - ta Love in Ne - vad - a
Dm7♭5
G7
Cm7
111
Just wait - in' for you! So come to Las Ve - gas!
8vb

114
C♯dim7
TOMMY:
What'd I say?
B♭6/D
Fm/G
BUDDY:
Lead the way
G7♯5
ALL 3:
To Las
8vb
117
Cm9
Ve - gas!
B♭
Cm
B♭/D
E♭6
E6
F13
E13
F13
The land
120
N.C.
where dreams
B♭6
come
B♭7/D
true.
E♭
C7/E
F7
123
TOMMY: Come on, Las Vegas!
B♭13
Yeah!
8va
sffz

OUT OF THE SUN

Music and Lyrics by
JASON ROBERT BROWN

11
Cm(Maj9)
D♭9
Cm(Maj9)
young, we don't know from im - pos-si - ble. We put our faith in mox - ie and ro -
14
D♭9
A♭Maj9
D♭7
mance, But when it's ripped a - way, tossed out the door, it strips your
17
E♭Maj7/B♭
A♭6
D 7♭9
3
in-no - cence right to the core, And soon you spend your time just wish - ing
20
G7sus
G
Cm9
F13
for A sec - ond chance.
a tempo

23
B♭m9
G♭13♯11
F7♯5
B♭m9
I nev - er knew– I nev - er
26
G♭13
B♭m9
E♭m7
guessed That what could kill you is the thing you love the best. I should have
29
Cm7♭5
Cm7♭5/F
F7
B♭m9
got-ten her out of the sun.
32
G♭9♯11
Fm7(add4)
F7♯5(♭9)
B♭m9
G♭13
When she re - clined, clouds dis-ap - peared. She smelled like

35
B♭m9
E♭m7
Gm7♭5
co-co-nuts from all the oil she shmeared! I should have got-ten her
38
B♭m/C
C7
FMaj9
out of the sun! But she was
41
D♭Maj9
G♭13
A♭Maj7/E♭
beau-ti-ful, be-yond com-pare, Roast-ing like a chick-en in her
44
C7♭5(♭9)
Fm9
B♭7sus
B♭7
chair. Look at how the col-or of her hair Chang-es as the

47
B♭m7/E♭
D 7♭9
D♭Maj9
day burns on.
She wore no Cop-per-tone, She wore no
50
G♭13
A♭Maj7/E♭
C 7♯5(♭9)
hat! The doc-tors swore they nev-er saw skin look like that, Like a
53
Fm(Maj9)
B♭7
Fm(Maj9)
sad-dle-bag. Oo, sad-dle-bag...
56
E♭/F
F9
B♭m9
G♭9♯11
I was a fool– So blind and deaf. I might have

59
B♭m9
E♭m7
Cm7♭5
saved her with a high-er S. P. F.,
But now she's
gone!
What's past is
62
Cm7♭5/F
F7
B♭m9
Gm7♭5
past!
What's done is
done!
Could I feel
65
G♭Maj13
E♭m6/F
rot-ten-er?
I wish I'd
got-ten 'er
Out of the
69
B♭m(Maj9)
sun.

FOREVER STARTS TONIGHT

Music and Lyrics by
JASON ROBERT BROWN

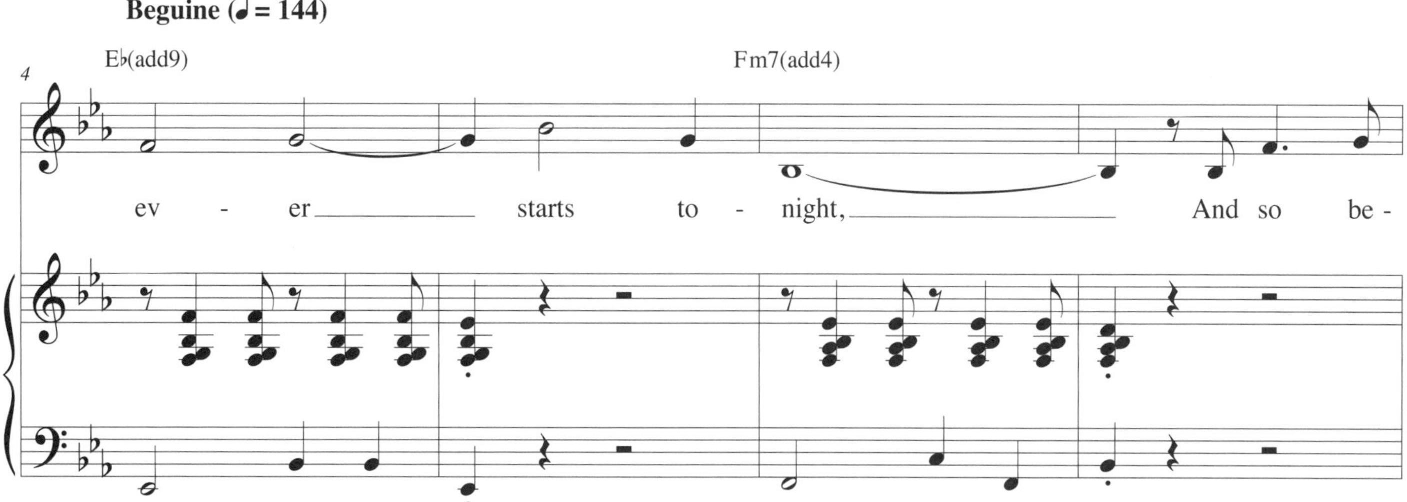

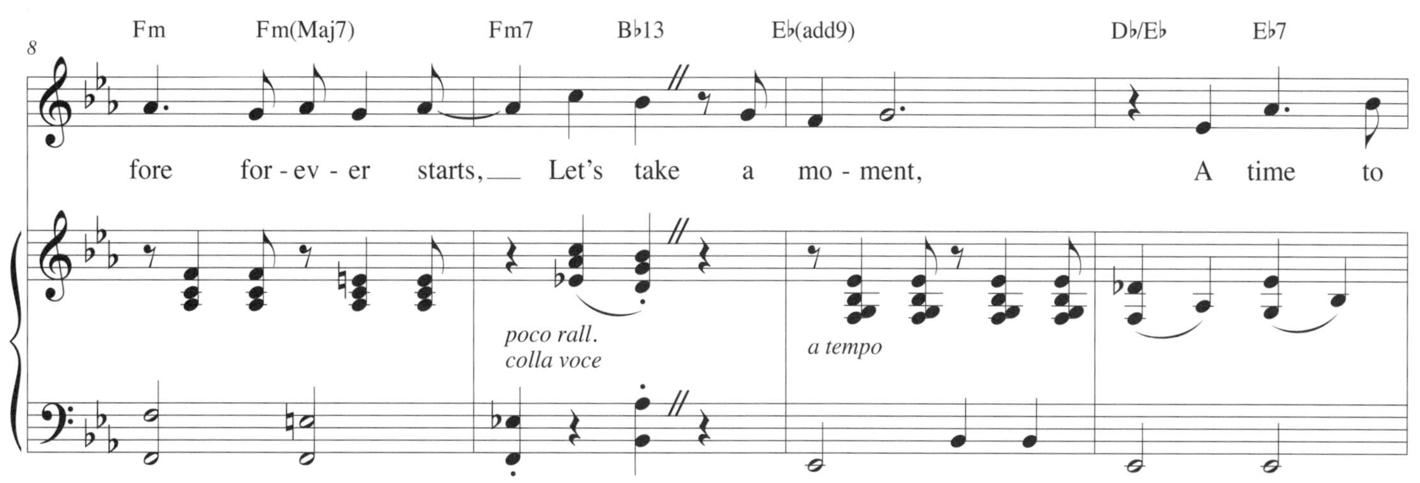

12
A♭ A♭/G Fm7 B♭7 Gm7♭5 C7
3 3
med - i - tate on what for - ev - er means, Each in our
16
Fm7 A♭/B♭ B♭♯5
own way, Each a - lone. For -
20
E♭Maj9 E♭6/9 Fm7(add4) B♭7
ev - er starts to - night, But if there's
24
Fm Fm(Maj7) Fm7 B♭ E♭Maj9 D♭/E♭ E♭7
3
one thing I would Wish be - fore it start - ed, I'd want the

28
A♭ Cm7/G Fm7 B♭7 Gm7♭5 C7
chance to tell my sin - gle life good - bye, Smok - ing a
32
Fm7 Fm7/B♭ D♭/E♭ E♭7
sto - gie, Play - ing some cards...
36
A♭ B♭/E♭ E♭6
Get a man - i ped - i and a Thai mas - sage!
f
40
Am7♭5 D♭7♭9 Gm
Find the pool, get start - ed on your tan!

44
Cm7
F7
B♭
E♭m/B♭
B♭
3
Go to the ca - si - no, Give the wheel a spin, Get your
3
8vb
48
Am7♭5
D7♯5(♯9)
GMaj9
B♭7♯5
shop - ping in While you can, Be - cause for -
52
E♭Maj9
E♭6/9
Fm7(add4)
B♭7
ev - er starts to - night, And then you're
mf
56
Fm
Fm(Maj7)
Fm7
B♭
E♭Maj9
D♭/E♭
E♭7
nev - er go - ing an - y - where with - out me, And you'll feel

A♭ Cm7/G Fm7 B♭7 Gm7♭5 C7
sil - ly that you ev - er thought to doubt me! We've_ got a
Fm7 Fm7/B♭ Gm7♭5 C7♯5(♯9)
life - time Of man - and - wife time, So what's an
Fm7 Fm7/B♭ Gm7♭5 C7
hour? We'll be all right, Un - til for -
Fm7 B♭5
ev - er starts... to -

76
E♭
D7
night!
81
G
A/D
D
TOMMY:
What could be the harm in such a friend - ly game?
f
85
G♯m7♭5
C♯7♭9
F♯m
Why de - ny a man his sim - ple fun?
89
Bm7
E7
A
Dm/A
A
JACK & TOMMY:
Thir - ty - sev - en shoe stores call - ing out your name
Spend, and
8vb

G♯m7♭5 C♯7♯5(♯9) F♯Maj7 A/B
93
JACK:
TOMMY:
JACK:
feel no shame! Get some sun! But not too much! Be-cause for-
3
EMaj9 F♯m7 B7
97
ev - er starts to - night, And once you're
F♯m F♯m(Maj7) F♯m7 B7 EMaj9 Bm7/E
101
JACK & TOMMY:
in my arms, We won't be torn a - sun - der! They may say,
A A/G♯ F♯m7 B7 G♯m7♭5 C♯7♭5
105
"How is she with him?" Well! Let 'em won - der! I just need
3

109
F♯m7
A/B
G♯m7♭5
C♯7♭9
one game, And then there's one dame I shall en -
113
F♯m7
A/B
G♯m7♭5
C♯7
deav - or to de - light When for -
117
F♯m7
B5
ev - er starts to -
121
E5
night!

BETSY'S GETTING MARRIED

Music and Lyrics by
JASON ROBERT BROWN

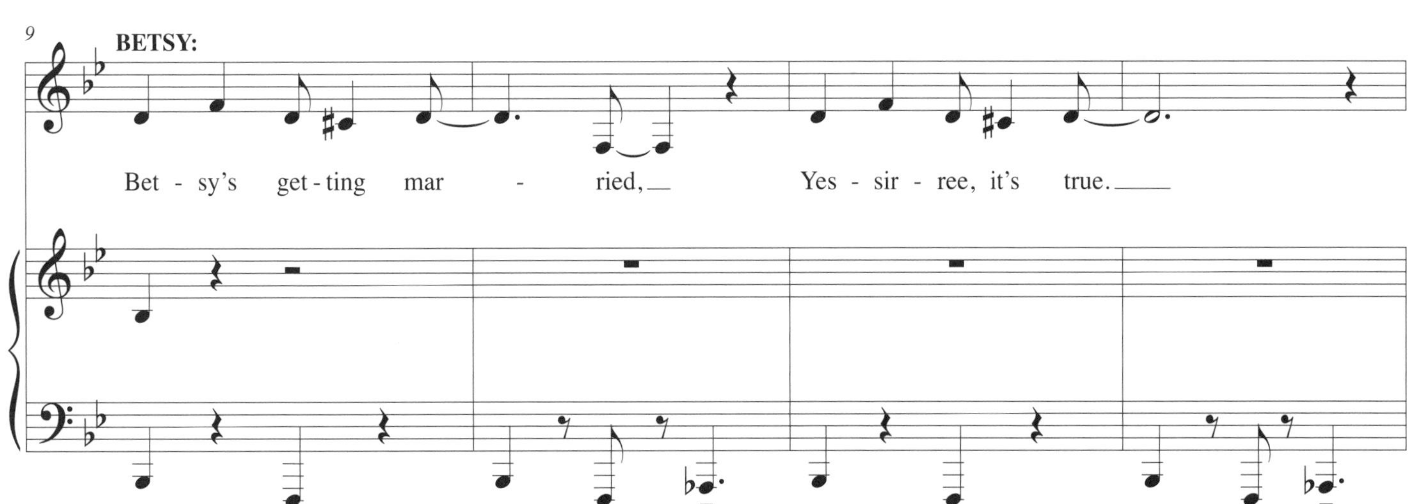

13
E♭13
Fi - nal - ly Jack got it through his head.
Bet -
17
B♭
G7♯5
- sy's get - ting mar - ried
Long past o - ver - due!
21
Cm7
C♯dim7
B♭6/D
G7♭5
G7
Thir - ty - one years of "hold - ing tight,"
And cross - ing my fin - gers ev - 'ry night,
You
25
Cm7
B♭/D
E♭
C7/E
E♭/F
bet - ter be - lieve I'm wear - ing white,
'Cause Bet - sy's get - ting

28
N.C.
F+/A
wed.
32
B♭6
D♭/A♭
B♭6
D♭/A♭
Bet - sy's get - ting mar - ried,
Call my col - lege gang!
36
B♭6
D♭/A♭
B♭6
Cm7
C♯dim7
B♭6/D
E♭13
E - ven though they gave me up for dead.
Bet -
40
B♭
G7♯5
- sy's get - ting mar - ried,
Get me Ve - ra Wang!

44
Cm7
C♯dim7
B♭6/D
G7♭5
G7
Thir-ty-one years I climbed that hill,
Sev-en-teen years I'm on the pill,
48
Cm7
B♭/D
E♭
C7/E
E♭/F
B♭
Li-sa Le-vine's on J-Date still,
But Bet-sy's get-ting wed.
53
E♭13
Ooh, ooh,
is-n't he smart and sweet and dream-y?
57
C7/E
Ooh, ooh,
don't I wish Mom and Dad could see me?

B♭6/F
Gm7
Ooh, ooh, all of these wan-na-bes wan-na be me! It
G♭7
C7♭5(♭9)
F7♯5
might be luck, it might be fate, But what-ev-er it is, it was worth the wait!
E♭13
BETSY & MEN:
Ooh, ooh, who is that prin-cess wear-ing Pra-da?
C9/E
Ooh, ooh, who is the toast of all Ne-vad-a?

77
B♭6/F
Gm7
BETSY:
Ooh, ooh, who's gon-na get the whole en-chi-la-da? He'll
81
G♭7
C7♭5(♭9)
F7♯5
be mine and I'll be his– It took for-ev-er but here it is!
85
B♭
MEN:
Bet-sy's get-ting mar-ried. Get that girl a drink!
89
Send that cou-ple break-fast in their bed!

E♭6
Edim7
B♭/F
G7♭5
G7
93
BETSY:
Thir-ty-one years I knit my brow,
Won-der-ing when and who and how.
Well,
sub. mp
97
Cm7
ba-by I hit the jack-pot now,
'Cause
f
101
E♭/F
MEN: Bet - sy!
Bet - sy's
BETSY:
get - ting
105
N.C.
wed!

COME TO AN AGREEMENT

Music and Lyrics by
JASON ROBERT BROWN

B7
D9
C♯7♭9
Look, I'm not with - out com - pas - sion. We could come to an a -
F♯m7
B7
Am/E
gree - ment, Or you could pay three grand a week.
A tempo, in 2
E
E♯dim7
F♯m7
B7
We could come to an a - gree - ment, There are dif - ferent things to
rall.
EMaj9
E6
E♯dim7
F♯m7
B13
try. We could come to an a - gree - ment, I'm an ea - sy - go - ing

G♯m7♭5
C♯7♭9
F♯m7
guy. You could have a hap - py land - ing
B7
D9
C♯7
If we had an un - der - stand - ing. We could come to an a -
In 4
F♯m7
B7
E
gree - ment, Or you can kiss your balls good - bye.
A tempo, in 2
A
G♯m7♭5
C♯7♭9
F♯Maj9
Some - times you need chal - leng - es to set you free. In ad - ver - si - ty, Peo - ple

36
F♯m7 B7 EMaj7 Em7 A13
grow. You said you were broke, ex - cept you were - n't, see? You've got
rall.
Poco rubato, slower, in 4
39
D6/9 C♯7sus(♭9) C♯7 F♯m/C♯
cur - ren - cy You don't know. When my Don - na died, my world blew in - to
42
C♯sus C♯7 F♯m/C♯ C♯sus C♯7
piec - es, Jack. When my Don - na died, a part of me died, too. And I
45
F♯m/C♯ C♯sus C♯7 F♯m/C♯
thought that I could leave her in the past, I tried, But I'm sit - ting here and wish - ing I was

In 2
48
F+
A/E
D/E
E7
you. I know it sounds bi - zarre, But
In 4
51
A/E
C♯7sus
C♯7
F♯m/C♯
things are what they are. I would like to spend the week - end with your
rall.
54
C♯sus
C♯7
F♯m/C♯
C♯sus
C♯7
girl - friend, Jack. I will be the per - fect gen - tle - man, I swear. Just a
57
F♯m/C♯
C♯sus
C♯7
F♯m/C♯
week-end, us a - lone, me and your girl - friend, Jack, Then we're set - tled and it's fin - ished. Fair is

60
In 2
F+
A/E
DMaj7
fair! Look, if you were all that eag - er to get mar - ried, Jack, Then you
63
A/C♯
Dm6
Slower, in 4
A/E
would - n't have been sit - ting in that chair. So what's a week - end? What's the
8va
66
A+/E♯
F♯m7
B7sus
B7
Mosso, in 2
E11
dif - f'rence? You've got lots of time to spare.
8va
70
C♯7♭9
Let's just come to an a -
rall.
5
8va
15ma

A tempo, in 2
F♯m7
B7
EMaj9
gree - ment.
Tell me what you want to do.
E6
C♯7♯5(♭9)
F♯m7
B7
We can come to an a - gree - ment. You've got op - tions: let's re -
G♯m7♭5
C♯7
A tempo, in 2
F♯m7
view.
You can owe me 'til you're strung out,
rit.
B7
D9
C♯7
Or have Vin - nie rip your tongue out,
Or we can come to an a -

A little slower, in 2
84
F♯m7
B7
A/B
E/B
gree - ment.
It's com-plete - ly up to you.
rall.
88
A/B
E/B
A/B
E/B
Does she love you, Jack?
Does she
92
A/B
E/B
B7
A♯m7♭5 B7
love you, Jack?
If she loves you, Jack,
Then we can come to an a-
rit.
colla voce
In 4
96
E♭6 E6 E♭6 E6 E♭6 E6
gree - ment.
sfz

FRIKI-FRIKI

Music and Lyrics by
JASON ROBERT BROWN

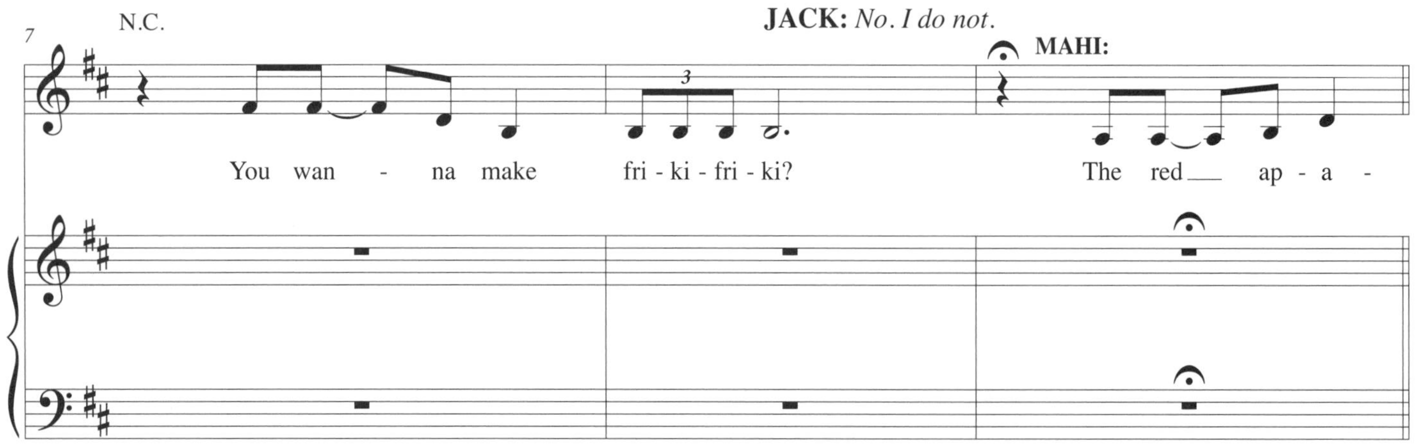

A little more
D6
N.C.
B7
N.C.
pa - ne
Is learn - ing to fly!
The spar - rows are
E7
A7 N.C.
JACK: Please start the car.
MAHI:
call - ing–
You wan - na make fri - ki - fri - ki?
A lo - cal tra -
Island Bossa Nova (♩ = 157)
B♭m7
G♭6
di - tion:
When-ev - er the my - na sings her song,
A man and a
C7♭5
F9
A7
wom - an
must touch in - stant - ly!
Take a look at the

26
D6
B9
ne - ne
That's pass - ing you by.
The red - foot-ed
30
E7
A7
F♯m7♭5
B7
boob - y!
Now who could de - ny
It's time to make
34
E9
GMaj7/A
4
wet and stick - y
fri - ki - fri - ki - fri - ki with
37
D6
A7
JACK:
me?
Bet - sy

Sweeping, poco rubato
D6
GMaj7
loves me. She's up - set, but Bet - sy loves me, And as soon as I can
45
D/F#
G
A/G
D/F#
G(add2)
G/A
A7sus
show her how I've changed, She'll for - get the whole me - gil - lah. Bet - sy
49
D6
GMaj7
Gm(Maj7)/B♭
loves me. Move your hand, please. Bet - sy loves me! And the
rit.
Back to island feel
53
A7
G/A
A7
G/A
birds are ver - y spe - cial here, it's true, But

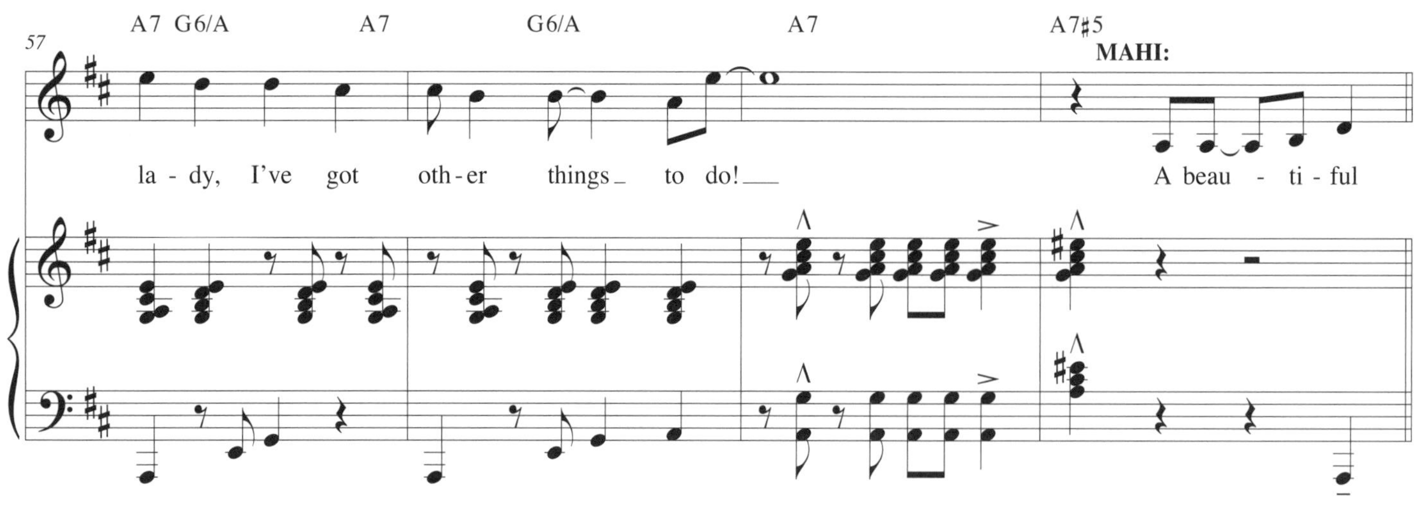
A7 G6/A
A7
G6/A
A7
A7♯5
57
MAHI:
la - dy, I've got oth - er things to do!
A beau - ti - ful

D6
B9
61
MAHI:
sun - set. The sound of the loon. Is it get-ting
JACK:
Please start the car. Please start the car.

E7
A7
D6
G♯dim A7
65
warm here? Come on, we make fri-ki-fri-ki! The churn of the
Don't take that off, please!

69
D6
B7
o - cean! The rise of the moon! The an - i - mal
73
E7
A7
D
C♯ D
yearn - ing! It's time to make fri-ki-fri - ki! There's no - bod-y
Rubato
77
B♭m7
G♭6
look - ing! Just o - cean a mil - lion miles long! Your spir - it is
(l.h.)
8va
81
C7♭5
F13
A7
scream - ing, So set your-self free! You wan-na see some
ff
(r.h.)

85
D6
B7
3
mo - e mo - e! You wan-na see some ha-na ma - 'i! You wan-na lit - tle la -
89
E9
A7
F♯m7♭5
B7
un - a 'a - na! Guess what? I a - gree! Come on and get a lit-tle
93
E9
A13
Wet and stick - y, Slurp - y, lick - y Fri - ki - fri - ki - fri - ki fri - ki
97
A+
D6
A13
D
With me!

A LITTLE LUCK

Music and Lyrics by
JASON ROBERT BROWN

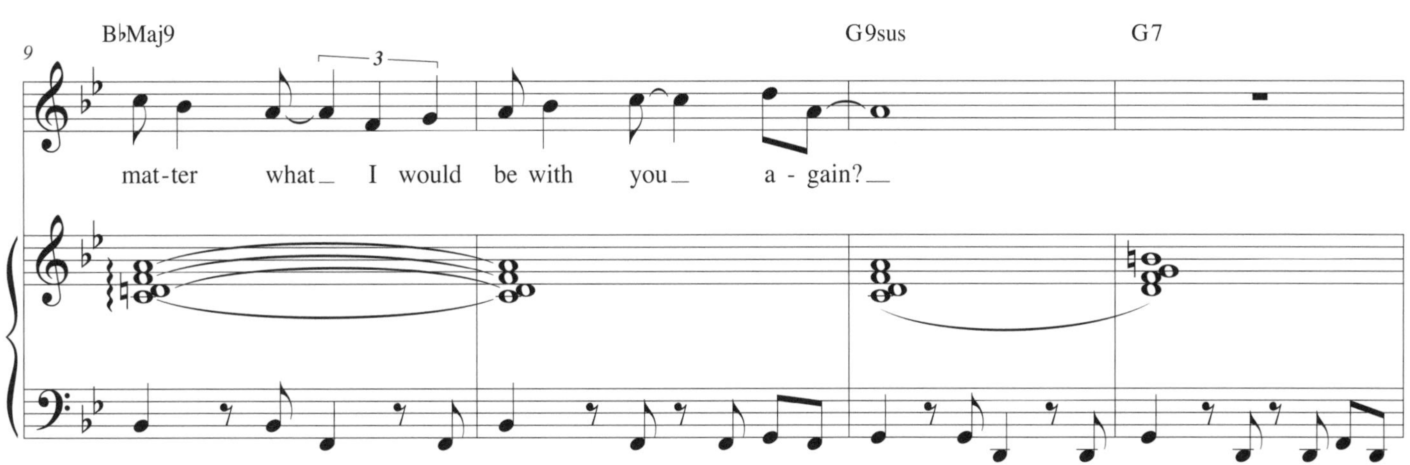

Gm7(add4)
C7♭9
Am11
A♭9♯11
G9
G7♭9/B
Cm9
(no breath)
Wow, Don-na– Can you be-lieve it's true? Is -
F9
F13♭9
E♭6/B♭
B♭6 N.C.
- n't it a-maz-ing what a lit-tle luck Can do?
B♭Maj9
E♭9♯11
B♭Maj9
Yes, Don-na. There by your side, I swore That I'd
G7sus
G7
make things just Like the way they were be-fore.

29
Gm7(add4)
Eb♭m7/C
Am11
A♭9♯11
Dm7/A
G7♭9
Cm9
(no breath)
Bam, ba-by! Ev-'ry-thing's good as new! Is-
33
F9
F13♭9
A♭6
A6
B♭6
Em7
-n't it a-maz-ing what a lit-tle luck Can do! Love
37
Am11
CMaj7/D
D13♭9
GMaj9
may be blind, but the stars Were a-ligned in my fa - vor. Sure,
41
Gm9
C13
C13♭9
FMaj9
I'm a pro, but let's face it, That's no guar-an-tee.

44
F♯m7
B13♯11
B9
Here's my tech - nique: I re - solve not To weak - en or
47
E6
EMaj9
E6
B♭m7
E♭7♭9
wa - ver– Then what is that fla - vor? Sweet vic - to-
51
A♭Maj13
G♭13
E♭m/F
F7♭9
(no breath)
B♭Maj9
ry! See, Don - na? Just like it used to be!
55
E♭13♯11
B♭Maj9
If some folks get hurt, Well, re - mem - ber, so did
mp

59
G9sus
G6
(no breath)
Gm7(add4)
C7♭9
we.
Now,
prin - cess,
Sit and en - joy the view!
63
Am7(add4)
A♭7♯11
G7sus
G7♭9
Cm9
Is - n't it a - maz - ing when you're
66
F13
F13/E♭
Dm7♭5
G13
G7♯5
Feel - ing stuck,
When you're in the muck,
When you're thun - der - struck
What a
69
Cm9
F13
F13♭9
B♭6
D7♭9 C7♭5 B♭9
lit - tle bit - ty bit of luck
Can do.

Am11 CMaj7/D D13♭9 GMaj9
Who'd ev - er bet __ that this pat - zer Would get __ to start o - ver? __
f
76
Gm7 C9 C13♭9
3
__ What __ are the odds __ that the gods __ Would give me __ one more __
79
F6/9 FMaj9 F6 F♯m7
__ chance? __ Who __ would sus - pect __ she would fall __
82
B13 B9♯5 EMaj9 E6 EMaj9 E6
3
3
__ For this wrecked __ Cas - a - no - va? __ Jump - in' Je -

B♭m7
E♭13
E♭13♭9
A♭Maj7
G♭9♭5
Fm7♭5
F9♯5
B♭Maj9
TOMMY & JOHNNY:
(no breath)
ho - vah!
Ba - by, let's
dance!
Well,
well,
well!
mp sub.
Ev - 'ry - thing's right on
track!
E♭13♯11
JOHNNY:
It was
mp
B♭Maj9
G9sus
G9
Gm7(add4)
TOMMY:
touch and
go,
But you
got
the
mag - ic
back!
A -
men,
broth - er!
C7♭9
And
mer - ci
beau - coup!
Am7(add4)
A♭7

G7sus
G7♭9/B
Cm9
F13
F13/E♭
100
JOHNNY:
TOMMY:
Is - n't it a - maz - ing what a well - placed buck... And some
mf
Dm7♭5
G7
G7♯5
G7
Cm9
103
JOHNNY:
BOTH:
well - trained pals... And a sit - ting duck... And a lit - tle bit - ty bit of luck
N.C.
F13
B♭6
B♭7/A♭
106
Can do!
f
B♭/G
E♭m/G♭
Cm7
B♭/D
E♭m6
Edim7
F7
B♭6
109

ISN'T THAT ENOUGH?

Music and Lyrics by
JASON ROBERT BROWN

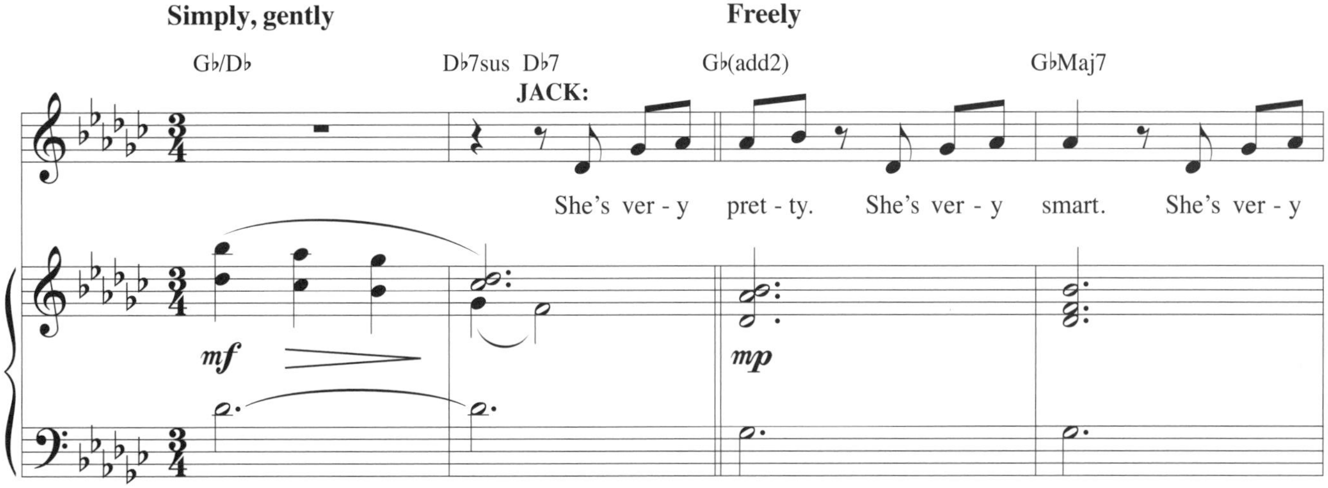

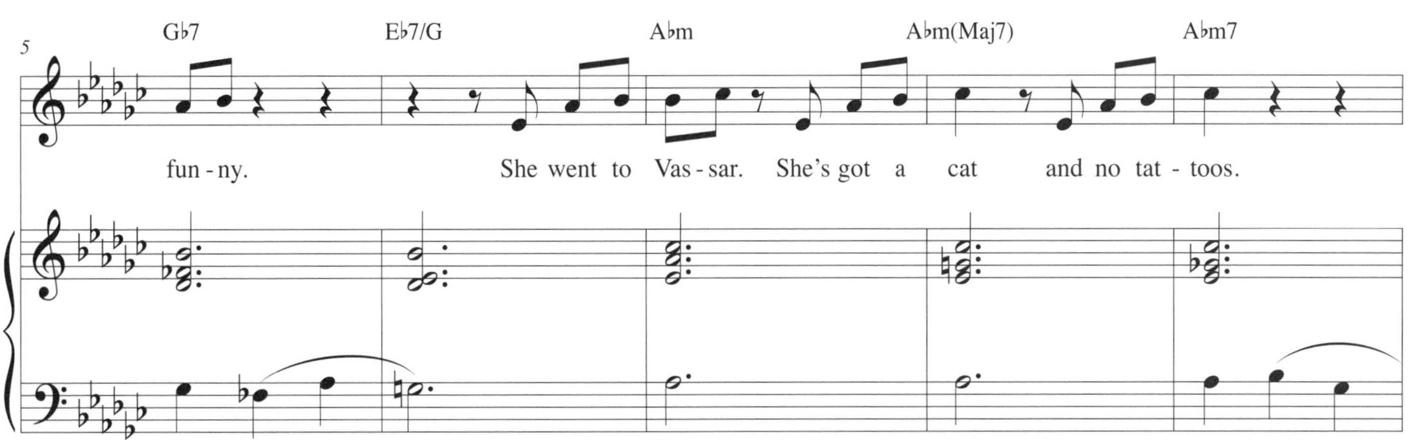

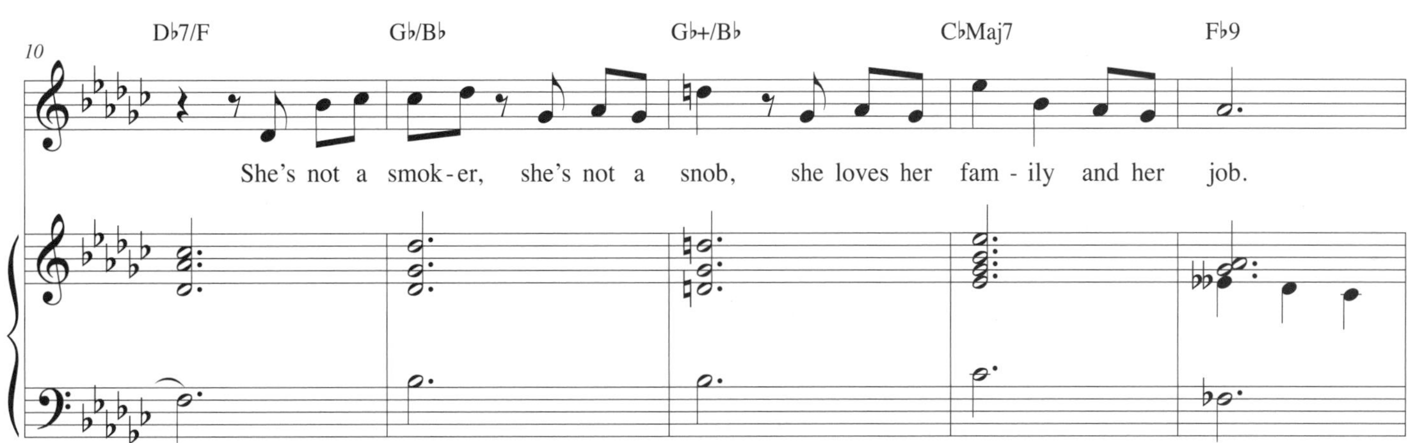

15
Gb/Db
Db7sus
Gb/Db
Db7sus
Db7
Is - n't that e - nough?
She likes my
A little more movement
19
Gb(add2)
GbMaj9
Gb9
Eb7
cook - ing. At least she tries. She thinks I'm fun - ny. When I get
23
Abm
Abm(Maj7)
Abm7
Db7
Db7/Cb
cra - zy, she ne - ver cries, We work things through. And she in -
27
Gb/Bb
Gb+/Bb
CbMaj7
Fb9
spires me like no one does. She makes me bet - ter than I was.

31
G♭/D♭ D♭7sus D♭7 C♭m/G♭ G♭
Is - n't that e - nough for you? Let's face it,
35
E♭m9 C♭(add2) E♭m9 C♭(add2) E♭m9
I don't know when I'll get that luck - y a - gain. She is-n't you, Mom, but then
40
A♭7/C D♭7sus D♭7 G♭/B♭
who could be? I was a mor - on. I was a
44
G♭+/B♭ C♭Maj7 F♭9 G♭/D♭
hack, and if she'll just take me back, that would be e - nough for

Poco mosso
49
G♭
G♭maj7
G♭7
E♭7
me.
mp
53
A♭m
A♭m(Maj7)
A♭m7
D♭7
Ddim
JACK:
You left a
57
E♭m9
C♭Maj9
E♭m9
C♭Maj9
long time a - go.
I was a boy then, you know.
And Bet - sy
mf
Broadening
61
E♭m9
A♭9/C
C♭/D♭
D♭7
helped me to grow, hope - ful - ly.
I turned the

65
G♭/B♭
G♭+/B♭
C♭Maj7
F♭9
cor - ner, I'm off the fence. She makes my whole world make sense, and
rit.
69
G♭/D♭
D♭7sus
G♭/D♭
D♭7sus
D♭7/C♭
ma - ma, that's e - nough.
pp a tempo
73
G♭/B♭
D♭7sus/C♭
D♭7sus
D♭7
G♭
G♭+
Ma - ma, that's e - nough for me.
mp rit.
p a tempo
77
C♭Maj9
C♭m(Maj7)
G♭/D♭
G♭(no5)
rit.
p

HIGHER LOVE

Music and Lyrics by
JASON ROBERT BROWN

Elvis "Boogie" (♩ = 170)

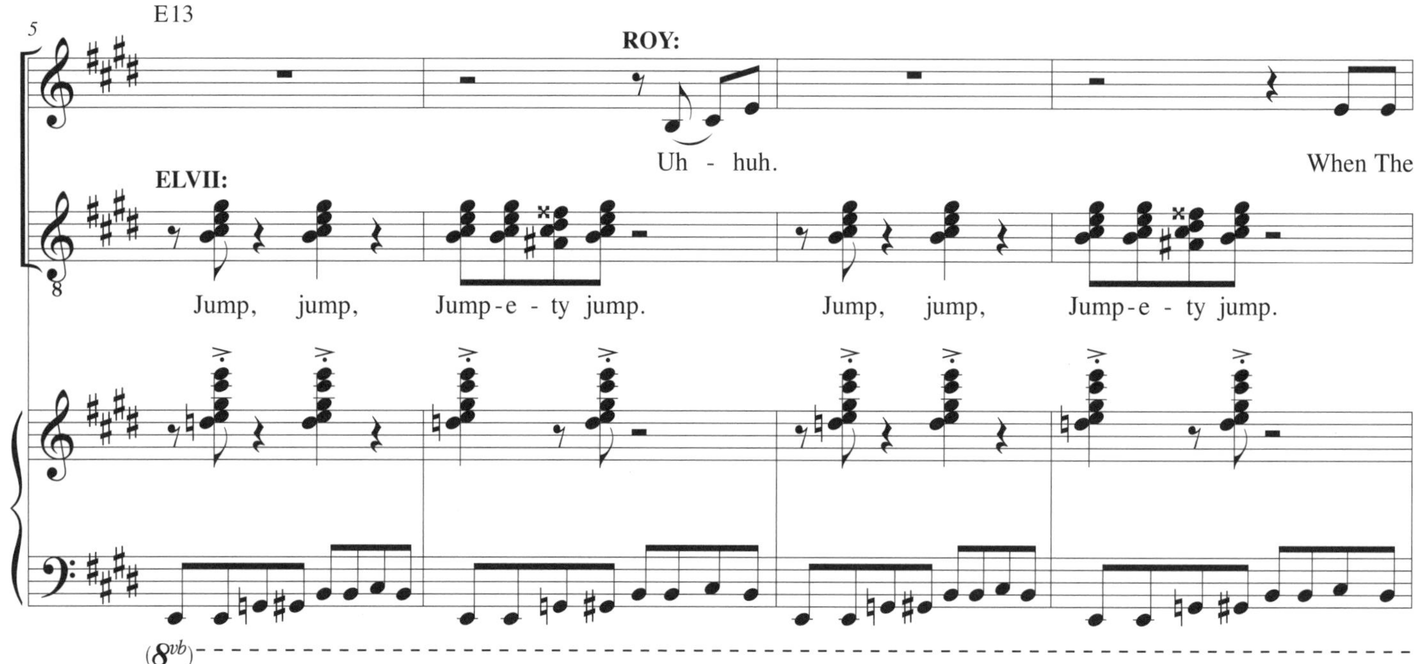

12
But I knew, like a flash, like a bolt of light-nin', that his
(8vb)
15
G7
sto-ry must be told. So I trad - ed my dog for an
(8vb)
18
old gui-tar And I taught my-self how to sing, And from that
(8vb)
21
E6
A/B
day to this, I have lived my life In the ser-vice of The King!
(8vb)

24
E13
Uh - huh.
Jump, jump, Jump - e - ty jump. Jump, jump,
f
(8vb)
27
E7
I curled my lip, I learned to shake my hip, I bought a
Jump - e - ty jump.
mf
(8vb)
30
Nu - die suit all in white, But I felt in my gut, in my
(8vb)

33
bones, in my heart, that some-thin' just was-n't right, So I got
Uh - huh!
(8vb)
G7
36
on my knees, I said, "El - vis, please you got to tell me what to do!"
(8vb)
39
E7
And a light shone down and a
(8vb)
41
A/B
heav-en-ly voice said, "Roy, I'm talk-in' to you!"
(8vb)

43
E/B Eb/B D/B Eb/B E/B Eb/B D/B Eb/B
ROY:
He said,
Ah!
Ah!
f
loco
47
E D/E E D/E E D/E E D/E
"Love is nev - er eas - y, Roy.
mp
51
E D/E E D/E E
Love is nev - er clear.
ENSEMBLE: (at pitch)
Ah ah ah!

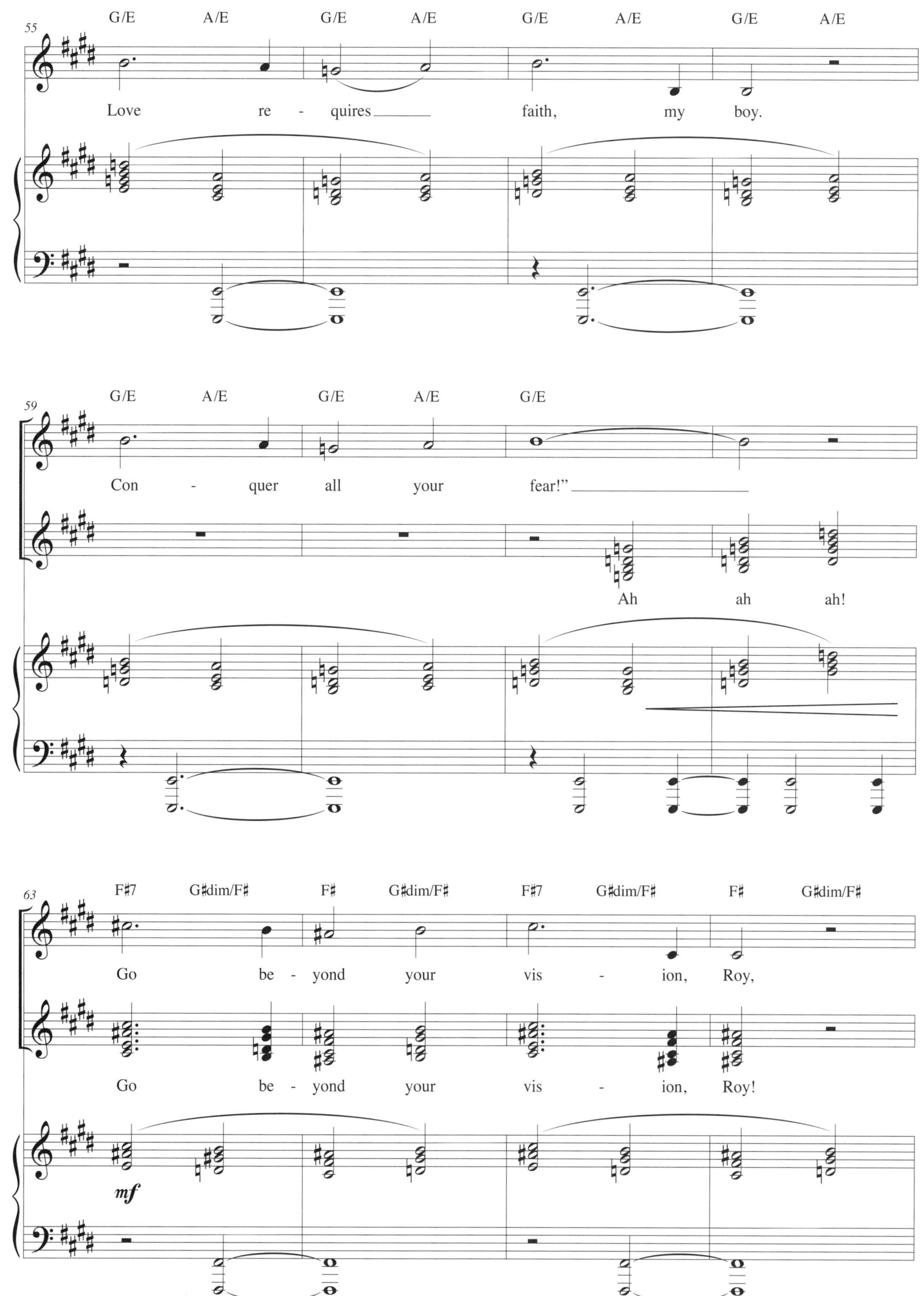
55
G/E A/E G/E A/E G/E A/E G/E A/E
Love re - quires faith, my boy.
59
G/E A/E G/E A/E G/E
Con - quer all your fear!"
Ah ah ah!
63
F♯7 G♯dim/F♯ F♯ G♯dim/F♯ F♯7 G♯dim/F♯ F♯ G♯dim/F♯
Go be - yond your vis - ion, Roy,
Go be - yond your vis - ion, Roy!
mf

67
F♯7
G♯dim/F♯
F♯
G♯dim/F♯
F♯7
Look in - to the sky!
Ah ah ah
71
Bm7/F♯
Take a chance and take that leap and
Ah! Ah ah!
f
75
B7
A(add2)/B
fly!
Fly!
mf

Bm7♭5
N.C.
B7
79
Fly!
Un-til you feel that
ff
83
A7
E7
E13
ROY:
High - er love!"
ENSEMBLE: (at pitch)
High - er love!
f
85
A7
E13
A7
Talk-in' 'bout a high - er love!
You could get all the rich-es you been
88
G9
dream - in' of, But you won't know what you're miss-in' If you

90
B7
A7
E7
don't know how to lis - ten for the High - er love!
ENSEMBLE: (at pitch)
High - er love!
92
E13
A7
E7
D9
A hunk o' hunk o' high - er love! I
8vb
95
C9
got the word from The King a - bove That a man ain't a man if he
(8vb)

98
B7sus
E13
can't feel the high - er love!
Uh - huh.
ENSEMBLE: (at pitch)
Jump, jump, Jump - e - ty jump.
(8vb)
101
Huh - huh.
Jump, jump, Jump - e - ty jump. Jump, jump,
(8vb)
104
BEAU:
Uh - huh.
I'm look - in' for a
Jump - e - ty jump. Jump, jump, Jump - e - ty jump.
(8vb)

107
A7
E7
A7
ROY:
High - er love!
Talk-in' 'bout a high - er love!

110
E7
A9
BEAU:
Some - times a guy needs a gen - tle shove, But you don't

113
G9
B7
A7
E7
get sump - in' If you can't start jump - in' for a High - er love!
ENSEMBLE: (at pitch)
High - er love!

116
E13
KYLE:
A7
E7
D9
ROY:
A hunk o' hunk o' high - er love!
You
8vb
119
KYLE, BEAU, & ROY:
C9
could knock boots with Cath - 'rine Den - euve, But you won't be a man If you
(8vb)
122
B7sus
E7
G7
can't feel the high - er love!
ENSEMBLE: (+ 8vb)
Lift me up, lift me up high - er!
mp sub.
(8vb)

125
E7
G7
E7
Lift me up, lift — me up high - er! Lift me up, lift —
128
G7
E7
G7
— me up high - er! Lift me up, lift — me up high - er!
131
F7
A♭7
F7
A♭7
Lift me up, lift — me up high - er! Lift me up, lift — me up high - er!
8va
mf
135
F7
A♭
F7
A♭
Lift me up, lift — me up high - er! Lift me up, lift — me up high - er!
(8va)

139
G7
Am/G
G
Am/G
G
ROY:
Love is not con - ven - ient, Jack!
loco
f
143
G
Am/G
G
Am/G
G
Kiss your fears good - bye!
ENSEMBLE: (at pitch)
Ah ah ah
3
147
Cm/G
Csus2/G
Get up off yer butt, my friend And
Ah!

151
C7
Bbsus2/C
fly!
Fly!
ENSEMBLE: (at pitch)
Fly!
Fly!
Fly!
Fly!
Fly!
Fly!
Fly!
Fly!
155
Cm7b5
C7
Fly!
You got-ta feel that
Fly!
Fly!
Fly!
Fly!
Fly!
8va
ff
159
Bb9
F7
Bb9
F7
High - er love!
Talk-in' 'bout a high - er love!
ENSEMBLE: (at pitch)
ff
High - er love!
Talk-in' 'bout a high - er love!

162
B♭9
F7
I tell ya it's a High - er love!
A
High - er love!
A
165
B♭9
F7
hunk o' hunk o' high - er love!
Give a lit - tle
hunk o' hunk o' high - er love!
167
B9
F♯7
B9
F♯7
High - er love!
I like a lick o' high - er love!
High - er love!
I like a lick o' high - er love!

170
E9
You try and you try just as hard as you can But you won -
mf
173
D9
C♯7♯5
- der why the shit keeps hit - tin' the fan, It's 'cause a man ain't a man Ain't a
8vb
176
N.C.
man ain't a man Ain't a man With - out the high - er love!
(8vb)
ff

179
F♯13
Jump, jump! Jump-e-ty jump! Uh-huh! Jump, jump!
182
Jump-e-ty jump! Uh-huh! Jump, jump! Jump-e-ty jump! Uh-huh!
185
N.C.
F♮9♯11
Huh!
sffz